# Capitalism Is Killing the Earth

## An Anarchist Guide to Ecology

# Capitalism Is Killing the Earth

## An Anarchist Guide to Ecology

First Edition, 2018

ISBN: 978-1-916-41290-3

Text by John Warwick with contributions from other Anarchist Federation members

Illustrations: Nicky Minus (pages 9, 14, 28, 36);

Guy Denning (page 22)

Cover image: Clifford Harper

Cover design: Euan Sutherland

Afed.org.uk

# Contents

# Glossary

Capitalism: An economic and political system based on the exploitation of those forced to sell their labour to survive. In this system, trade, industry and major decisions which affect the environment are made by private owners who are driven by profit.

Green capitalism: As above but with more solar panels.

Neoliberalism: A political system of free markets, privatisation of once communal resources and minimal regulations exploiting workers or the environment.

Scientific consensus: An agreement amongst the majority of experts in a field about a scientific process. Over 97% of climate scientists agree humans are causing climate change.

Holistic: An approach which assumes parts of a system are intimately interconnected and must be treated as a whole.

Colonialism: The practice of occupying a territory to exploit its natural resources and inhabitants.

Greenwash: Actions taken by politicians and corporations to appear 'green' and environmentally friendly whilst doing nothing of consequence.

The state: The collected institutions that create and enforce laws created by a small minority of people within a territory. Through laws the state claims that only it has the right to use violence. The state uses the law to justify and protect a capitalist economy.

MEDC/LEDC: More/Less Economically Developed Country

# Introduction

We are in a period of crisis that we in MEDCs cannot yet see. The signs are there if you look hard enough but at the moment the water is still flowing, the crops are still reliable, the ski lifts are still running. The first wave of climate refugees are trying to make their way into Europe but they are being dismissed as 'economic migrants' or those displaced by war. In all likelihood, MEDCs will not feel the effects of climate change for some time; our relative wealth will push the impacts onto those who haven't the means to adapt or whose local climates were less temperate to begin with. The longer we wait to act, however, the bigger the coming crunch will be.

Collectively, MEDCs are responsible for the overwhelming majority of cumulative carbon emissions and will have to radically change their energy and transport systems if an ecological disaster is to be avoided. Who will bear the brunt of the costs and who will get rich from this process is sadly predictable. The working class in MEDCs and most people in LEDCs will pay for the fossil fuel addiction and growth-at-all-costs model of the capitalist system. We have already begun to see this happen in the black, working-class communities devastated by natural disasters in the USA and flooding killing thousands in Bangladesh.

Capitalism relies on constantly increasing accumulation of profits. This has been achieved historically by appropriations (a polite term for thefts) both internal and external to the nation state. Internally, in Europe from the fifteenth century onwards, this has followed the model of stealing common land from the people to create a proletarian class dependent on wage labour to support itself. Externally, this expansion was tied to a move outside Europe's borders to exploit natural resources and labour in other locations. Thus colonialism and capitalism were, from the beginning, linked to processes of resource extraction and accumulation.

Capitalism is now in crisis; with so few areas beyond its reach, there are no easy sources of growth to appropriate, and the ability of the earth's ecosystems to accommodate further growth is being seriously questioned. How then to continue growth and profit? In MEDCs, we are seeing a fresh attack on workers' rights, with more precarious jobs, lower pay and poorer social care. In LEDCs, the neoliberal development model is pushed with privatisation and financial deregulation extracting the most profit for the capitalists.

We write this pamphlet to discuss the environmental problems that capitalism has created, with a focus on climate change and the false solutions offered up to us. There has been wider understanding of environmental issues since mainstream publications such as *Silent Spring, Gaia* and *An Inconvenient Truth*; however, an anti-capitalist critique has been lacking.

Capitalism is a system reliant on the total exploitation of nature; whether that be sacrificing our clean water to frack for hydrocarbons or sacrificing our children to the production line. We must develop our ideas of what a different future may look like outside the constraints of both capital and fossil fuels. We must also critique the false solutions offered by 'green capitalism' and increased state control. It is our contention that the world in fifty years will look radically different from what we see now. The question is whether we are moving towards a sustainable future for humanity, or one of catastrophe.

# Climate Change and Capitalism

The concept of human-caused climate change is not new. Joseph Fourier first discussed the greenhouse effect in 1824 and suggested human activities could influence global temperatures. Other famous names of chemistry and physics such as Tyndall, Arrhenius and Bell developed this theory and understood its implications. By the early twentieth century there was an understanding in the scientific community that burning fossil fuels could alter the earth's climate.

By the 1970s, public awareness of the issue had grown and the scientific community began to develop models of how $CO_2$ emissions would affect the future climate. During this period, the oil company Exxon conducted a great deal of research into climate change and global climate modelling. Their findings threatened the company's profits, so they suppressed the research and instead spent money on a misinformation and lobbying campaign to limit public acceptance and government regulation (see *Environmental Research* Letters: Bibliography). This was largely successful, with successive governments in the USA and elsewhere questioning the science of climate change and limiting regulation of $CO_2$, despite overwhelming scientific consensus. Misinformation of the public has been supported by many media outlets controlled by the ruling class, allowing governments to stall environmental regulation and treat climate change as a fringe issue.

In more recent times, we've seen even the right wing move from the climate denial of George W. Bush to the acceptance of environmental policy by the mainstream. For example, consider David Cameron's 'hug a husky' greenwash. Whilst greenwashing has conceded some small victories, many of the major global players are still delaying any meaningful action as far as possible, whilst promoting false 'green capitalism' solutions. Others have accepted climate change, but denied the human cause or that we can do anything about it. Donald Trump claimed in 2016 that climate change was a hoax promoted by China to weaken the economy of the USA, neatly bringing together both economic nationalism and climate denial. By painting the issue as one of national defence and economic necessity, Trump has managed to cast further doubt on the need to lower carbon emissions.

Environmental pollution is one of the great failures of the free market. Fossil fuels are cheap because $CO_2$ is a 'negative externality'; that is, the cost of emitting it, namely the threat of global environmental change, is not borne by the companies responsible but by society at large. Private companies, therefore, have little incentive to reduce $CO_2$ emissions, and the costs of their products are kept artificially low by this societal subsidy. These emissions have no market value – they add nothing to the cost of a product and yet have huge ramifications for the global climate. The market, therefore, cannot be relied on to fix this problem. The options available to us are to either control the market so that environmental costs are considered, e.g. state capitalism, or to remove the market's control over our lives altogether.

The longer we delay action on climate change, the more difficult to fix the problem becomes. This pamphlet proposes that the only way to achieve meaningful change is to abandon the capitalist model; to reclaim the energy and production systems from their corporate owners, and bring them into the hands of the people. This is no small task, but offers an escape from the multiple environmental disasters we currently face. We also point out that state power expands in times of crisis and, as such, we must be careful of solutions which increase the power of the state to control our lives. To achieve this, we must consider the maxim of 'think globally, act locally' and work towards decentralised solutions which give control of energy and production systems to the people who use them, for the benefit of the whole global ecosystem.

# Case studies: energy and housing under capitalism

## Energy Systems

In the current energy system we rely on privately owned, large-scale, centralised energy production, which removes from the consumer any say in how the energy is produced. Energy is delivered to the consumer for a fee with the profit margins of the producer regulated by the state, in exchange for the ability to operate as part of a small cartel. The true cost, however, is not considered. The environmental cost of emitting $CO_2$ in extracting and burning fossil fuels is not included in the price, making fossil fuels artificially cheap. This allows coal extraction and burning to continue because it remains profitable.

Energy systems are currently run for a dual purpose – to provide consumers with energy and to provide capitalists with profits. Future energy systems must be democratic in their control and operation. They need to serve their communities and focus on energy efficiency, thereby reducing demand and minimising environmental costs, rather than chasing profit. The technologies needed to achieve this should be tailored to the location. Wind and wave energy are more suitable in northern Europe, geothermal should be used where it occurs naturally, and solar in northern Africa.

In LEDCs, we need to avoid increasing carbon-intensive methods of living, which MEDCs have enjoyed since the industrial revolution. We need to improve the quality of life without relying on outdated and polluting technology. This is currently happening in a piecemeal fashion. However, much of the financing is provided by MEDCs as a method of offsetting their own carbon omissions.

We see an end to intellectual property rights as a mechanism of achieving this, so that low-carbon solutions can be transferred directly to the developing world. Demand can also be reduced through a rationalisation of industrial production, and a focus on the needs of the community rather than production for 'economic growth' or profit. We have the technology available to provide a clean energy system; what remains is to disseminate these ideas and technologies and take control for ourselves.

## Housing

The UK has some of the oldest housing stock in Europe, which is often draughty, uninsulated and poorly designed in terms of heating and energy efficiency. Many houses were built before heating's invention and single glazing is still common. The stock also has a very low turnover, as housing density is mainly low and houses are rarely demolished and replaced by their owners. This puts many renters in the situation of having to accept draughty homes that are expensive to heat and that suffer from problems of mould and damp.

As new houses are built, an opportunity arises to create homes which are energy-efficient and even carbon-neutral, producing energy through solar and wind installations at a home or community scale. This opportunity, however, is not being taken up, due to the market's unwillingness to pay a premium for energy-efficient homes. Developers, therefore, maximise their profit at the expense of the environment, by mostly building homes that need the usual fossil fuels for heating and are dependent on the current model of centralised, carbon-intensive energy networks. This locks us into this model for decades to come, or puts the cost of retrofitting on future generations. Zero carbon homes are possible with current technologies but they are not profitable enough for developers to build at scale. Creating homes with low energy demand and the ability to produce their own energy can allow people an increased level of self-sufficiency and the ability to meet the rest of their needs through community-scale renewable energy schemes.

There is approximately £837 billion worth of housing in the 'private rental sector', meaning that it is rented out for profit to people in need of a home. While this housing remains in the hands of investors we will not see rents lowered,and we will not see energy efficiency brought to the standard needed to avoid climate change. The decisions on how buildings are designed, run (and the appliances which go into them) are made, in large, by property developers who have few environmental constraints and only the profit motive to guide them. Ultimately, we must move to a system where our environmental fate and general wellbeing is decided by ourselves, with our own and our community's interests at heart. Sadly, however, when so many people are struggling to afford *any* home to live in, energy efficiency will remain a low priority.

## Resource depletion

Climate change is not the only problem facing the environment. We are consuming non-renewable resources at an alarming rate and pushing semi-renewable resources, such as fish stocks, to the point of collapse. As a society, we are treating these resources as if they are infinite, despite very strong evidence to the contrary. We mine rare earth metals for personal electronics, phosphorus for fertiliser, and oil for petrochemicals. All of these are occurring at unsustainable rates because nature is economically 'cheap'. The cost of a product to a consumer is simply the cost of extracting the resource plus the capitalist's profit; there is no consideration of the opportunity cost of consuming a finite resource now in a way that means it will be unavailable for future generations. Again, we have a problem of a negative externality. The extra costs of living in, for example, a phosphorous-limited world are not being born by the companies over-exploiting resources today but are being pushed onto future generations. Short-term increases in profit, growth and consumption are being prioritised over the stability of ecosystems and the availability of scant resources in the future.

From Texas to Uttar Pradesh, water resources are being over-exploited, either by farmers pumping groundwater to irrigate their crops in arid environments or by factory owners using it for industrial processes. In a capitalist system the farmers compete against each other and must secure as much water as possible for their own farms to maximise profits. They are also driven to produce the crops that will make them the most money, even if they deplete local resources. The net result is the depletion of groundwater so that wells either run dry or the cost of pumping water to the surface becomes too expensive. This is a classic example of the tragedy of the commons, whereby a communal resource is destroyed due to overuse by competing actors.

These kinds of problems are solvable and in fact Elinor Ostrom won a Nobel Prize in economics for her work on how the commons can operate harmoniously. Her work highlighted the need for strong community networks that could work together to create their own rules over how communal resources could be shared. In this way the best outcome for both individual and community can be achieved and the resource is preserved for future generations. This is almost the exact opposite of the capitalist system where neighbours act as competitors and must fight to ensure they receive as much as possible despite the impact on the commons itself. Within a capitalist system these communal resources are doomed by overuse, enclosure and destruction.

Many of the resources required in the silicon age are harvested far from the regions that are dependent on them. As resources become scarce in the future, we can expect this to become an increasing source of conflict, as governments and corporations try to control the supply. This has already occurred most explicitly in the Iraq War, which was used to secure access to oil, but it also occurs less overtly in the support of regimes which allow, or are forced to agree with, free trade and limited labour laws so that capital can exploit these resources cheaply. Here capitalists from MEDCs work hand-in-hand with their counterparts in LEDCs to ensure gains in workers' rights can be bypassed through outsourcing. This outsourcing of labour also occurs with carbon emissions and other forms of environmental degradation as 'dirty' jobs are shifted to regions with lower environmental regulations, allowing rich nations to appear to be lowering their emissions.

The global superpowers need to secure access to resources to keep their citizens insulated from future climate shocks and thus ensure political stability. In many cases this is taking the form of land grabs which are displacing local communities or forcing them into precarious labour. The Chinese state, for example, is buying up large tracts of Africa, the global implications of which we are yet to fully understand. For the USA and European states, this same process is taking place but through corporate proxies buying the land. When scarcity bites, it is likely that local populations resisting the export of needed resources will become hotspots for conflict against capital and the state. This new form of economic colonialism must be resisted.

Land ownership is also key as it, alongside perverse market forces, dictates how land is used and managed. Not all greenhouse gas emissions come from burning fossil fuels; many come from $N_2O$ released from fertiliser use in agriculture, methane from anaerobic processes in waterlogged soils, or simply from soil organic matter decomposing. These types of emissions are dependent on the way the land is managed. Again, in the current capitalist model there is little concern for the long-term health of the soil and no cost to the producer for emitting $N_2O$, methane or $CO_2$. While some forms of land degradation, such as clearing rainforests for cattle using slash and burn, are immediately obvious, some are less so. It can take generations before the soil becomes exhausted. These kinds of problems are most difficult to deal with when capitalists are trying to maximise short-term profits or when farmers are struggling to get by and cannot afford to consider the impact of their agricultural methods. We need, therefore, a holistic approach where all inputs and potential sources of environmental damage are considered and the land is held in common for the benefit of the whole community, as well as future generations.

Where we need to continue to use non-renewable resources, we need to work towards the creation of a circular economy where the waste of one product is used as the input for the next. This is starting to occur now but at a painfully slow rate due to the negative externality, which gives little economic incentive to do so, as discussed earlier. This will surely change as we approach peak production of oil, peak phosphorous and other resource limitations, but these resources are currently being used in such a reckless manner that we are severely disadvantaging future generations. We can manage limited resources effectively but only through production for need rather than for profit, as well as a return to the commons and the creation of a truly circular economy.

# False Solutions

Most proposals for change do not question the overarching system of capitalism and the market economy. The existence of private property, the appropriation of nature as a source of growth and production for profit instead of need are at the root of the problem, so they cannot be part of the solution. In this section we discuss the solutions offered by both capitalists and 'left' or 'green' political parties, as well as how they fail to address (or only partially solve) the problems we face.

## Climate summits and national carbon budgets

There have been numerous international climate summits but very little has been agreed as a result of them, and even less actually implemented. Most world leaders are unwilling to sacrifice the economic growth of their nation, even if it is to secure the long-term future of the species. Election cycles are a lot shorter than climate cycles and so politicians find it easy to dodge the issues and focus on short-term popularity with their financial backers and voters. Carbon budgets set at these summits are designed to have very little impact on the industries of the nations involved. They set a laughably low bar, which allows 'business as usual' with little interruption to the rate of emissions. Very little can be achieved at these summits for the simple reason that the needs of the planet's ecosystems do not align with the motivations of capitalists, whose opinions are put forward by their parliamentary representatives. There are a few notable exceptions to this rule, but these are largely from capitalists who have invested heavily in cleaner technologies, and thus stand to gain from a shift away from fossil fuels.

While climate summits do bring some periodic publicity to the issue, they also reinforce a state-centric model of change, which disempowers communities and encourages people to wait for progress from above. We can use these moments of media publicity to our advantage, but it would be a mistake to assume politicians will act in the interests of the planet as a whole, rather than the economic interests of their backers.


## Carbon trading and carbon capture

Carbon capture and storage promises to allow the continuation of a fossil fuel-based economy by capturing $CO_2$ released, and storing it underground. At present this technology has not been proven at large scale, and there are question marks over the stability of the $CO_2$ that is stored. The capture and storage of $CO_2$ also uses a considerable amount of energy itself, creating more inefficiency and waste. Even if the technology works, it does not address the fact that global reserves of fossil fuels are limited; it just allows us to continue using them until they run out, at greater levels of inefficiency, postponing the inevitable switch to renewable energy.

Carbon trading aims to cap the total amount of $CO_2$ that can be released by the world economy, while allowing flexibility by allowing companies and nations to trade their allowance of $CO_2$ emissions. The main problem with this is that it allows corporations and countries to continue emitting large amounts of $CO_2$, just as long as they have the cash to buy the permits to do so. This creates further inequality between those who can pay and those who can't, allowing consumption to continue in rich areas at the expense of the poor. Some corporations will simply find loopholes or illegally produce more emissions, by hiding them from regulatory authorities or bribing those in charge. The case of Volkswagen diesel emissions is perhaps the most famous recent example of this behaviour. There have also been problems reaching agreements on how a trading system would work and setting a price of carbon which actually affects corporate behaviour. The overall effect of a trading scheme is to slow the rate of change by allowing the big polluters to buy their way out of the problem instead of reducing their emissions.

## Green and ethical capitalism

If the subjugation of the working class is solar powered, does it make it any better? Green capitalism hopes to replace fossil fuels with renewables, whilst leaving the overall system in tact. Although this might help in the short term, it does not address over-consumption, the production for profit rather than need, resource depletion, over-fishing or mass extinctions. This proposed solution completely ignores capitalism's drive to produce more and more in order to drive up profits, always pushing at the limits of available energy and resources. This over-production can take many forms, from consumer goods made to need regular replacing, to vast standing armies with huge technological and industrial resources devoted to them.

A significant proportion of current emissions comes from this military industrial complex and, until recently, armies were exempt from reporting emissions. This meant that the US military could hide that it is responsible for approximately 5% of global emissions. During times of war, emissions from militaries increase dramatically, not to mention the human cost as well as the resources needed to rebuild homes and infrastructure after the war is over. See *The Green Zone: The Environmental Cost of Militarism* for more discussion.

If we address these issues of where production is targeted at the same time as we attempt to replace fossil fuels, we will find the total energy requirement of our society decreases, making the shift to renewable energy easier to manage. Even if green capitalism can help us in the short term, the next ecological crisis will always be just around the corner if we continue under this system. In fact, the provision of cheap and plentiful renewable energy systems could hasten other resource consumption as energy ceases to be the limiting factor.

Where small changes are happening to ecologically sound energy systems, capital is demanding public subsidy to underwrite the schemes, ensuring private gain at public risk. Many states are now torn between the vast resources of big oil, the emerging growth markets of green energy and public opinion. As a result, most MEDCs have defaulted to a compromise position, which allows business as usual for oil whilst also offering enough subsidies to provide 'green growth' to the economy and placate the public. Where green schemes interfere with capital, however, this is not tolerated. A recent example of this can be seen in the UK central government stepping in to overrule local councils that decided against fracking in their region. Tax revenues from the new shale gas boom were given priority over local communities.

We can expect capitalists and the state to use the many crises created by climate change as an opportunity to increase their control over the working class. This will likely occur by both socialising the costs of adaptation whilst privatising the profits, as well as through increased authoritarianism and nationalism, justified by the need to manage the crisis and keep the flows of climate refugees out. The climate crisis is already creating instability in food prices that has led to civil unrest across the globe; the capitalist class will not be the ones to feel the sharp end of these problems as they will always be able to pass the costs on to their workers and use their wealth to insulate themselves from any shortages.

Furthermore, calls for green or ethical consumerism are also deeply flawed, as the carbon footprint of rich consumers is dramatically higher than that of the poor, whether they consume 'green' products or not. Many so called 'green' products are only marginally better than the product they are replacing and act as an excuse for continued high levels of consumption, rather than producing an overall net reduction in emissions. This lifestylism allows wealthy people living in MEDCs to assuage their guilt and feel they're 'doing their bit' whilst, in many cases, compounding the issue or simply shifting the location of the emissions or pollution to LEDCs, where resources and labour are cheap.

## State control

Historically the state has acted as a mediator between capital and nature. It has provided the legitimacy required for capital to own and profit from nature through acts of enclosure, sale of public land and the eradication of the commons. Once it had achieved this it offered up further services to capital by enforcing property rights with its police force and judicial system, ensuring that no one could challenge the right to own nature. In the modern era the state at first tried to control the flows of capital across its geographic borders through taxation and duties, but more recently 'free trade' has prevailed. Now the state's role has retreated to simply providing the rights and permits that legitimise the further enclosure of nature. Where necessary the state has also helped tame nature for capital, providing the infrastructure, at public expense, that allows expansion to new markets, puts barren land into use and gets employees to work on time.

In planned economies with greater state control, such as China, we are seeing a rapid change in energy policy and action on $CO_2$ as the state can dictate the energy mix to a greater degree. China has the fastest growing solar industry in the world and is installing renewable energy sources at an impressive rate. This top-down approach, however, comes with its drawbacks. Large-scale hydropower has become a key part of the energy mix in China leading to the displacement of millions who were living in the areas now underwater above dams. This had also led to the extinction of numerous species of aquatic life. For the people living in these regions there was little that could be done to stop projects like the Three Gorges Dam. Scientists working on the project allege their environmental impact studies were doctored before being presented to planning committees.

With state planning come the usual disadvantages: centralisation of large schemes, no direct ownership or management by local communities and increased power for the state apparatus itself. States have always acted in their own interests, and those of the capitalists they represent, rather than in the interests of the people they rule, or of the planet itself.

## The divestment movement

The fossil fuel divestment campaign seeks to pressurise companies and governments to take action by making $CO_2$ emissions the next item on the responsible capitalism agenda. The divestment tactic is based on the fallacy that divestment can raise the cost of capital for the fossil industry and thus limit further exploration or extraction. This is simply not the case – many fossil fuel companies are not publicly traded and those that are do not raise money through issuing new shares. Also, the movement ignores the fact that for every public body divesting from fossil fuels there is also consequently a buyer of the shares investing in fossil fuels. All that changes is who receives company dividends and who gets a vote at the AGMs.

Around 70% of oil reserves are owned by states or nationalised state companies (e.g. Saudi Arabia, Iran, Norway, Qatar) so the main targets of divestment, such as Shell and BP, are actually only small parts of global oil production. In the current capitalist system where economic actors compete for limited resources there is no place for environmental concerns. The owners of fossil fuel reserves are incentivised to produce as much as possible before any potential legislation stops them. At the same time they will try their hardest to limit or delay any such legislation. This is where the divestment movement fails in its aims – it cannot succeed in constraining fossil fuel use without addressing both the huge reserves in state hands and a system that allows the wealthy elite to control environmental and economic policy for its own gain.

The movement has had some success in bringing awareness of climate issues to campuses and religious institutions. Action is needed on campus as many universities offer courses tailored to the fossil fuel industry despite the necessity of oil and coal extraction ending in the very near future; fossil fuel companies can maintain a veneer of legitimacy by partnering with academia. Divestment, then, can be a useful tool in building a movement around climate change. However, it is also a movement that has set goals that are unlikely to influence fossil fuel extraction in any meaningful way. Furthermore, by calling for reinvestment in green technologies the divestment campaign reiterates the green capitalist programme.

## Primitivism and Technology

In the face of ecological catastrophe and the destruction of habitats all over the world, some propose a return to more 'primitive' societies, such as subsistence agriculture, or a nomadic hunter-gatherer existence. They argue that complex societies of any kind will always be destructive and we should therefore abandon the use of nearly all technology. Whilst this does seem like a simple way of solving many environmental problems, it has many issues of its own. It would prevent many people across the world from maintaining or increasing their standard of living. Most damning of all, it would require the current population to be devastated in order for the number of people to be reduced to a level where it would be viable. Many of its proponents freely admit this, along with the fact that those of us who rely on medical technology would be left to deteriorate or die.

Ultimately, we as anarchists want to create a world without work, not a world of constant toil and struggle to survive. We want to be free to live comfortable lives and give ourselves the freedom to pursue the endeavours we choose: art, science, sport, travel and more. An overhaul of our energy and production systems can allow us to use technology without wrecking the environment.

The opposite extreme, that of a reliance on some future technological magic bullet yet to be developed has many of its own problems. It is used by many capitalists to justify a continuation of 'business as usual', doing nothing but waiting and hoping in the face of environmental collapse. Science and technology will certainly be part of any solution, but without accompanying economic and political changes they would very likely be used to increase the exploitation and inequality in our society. Technology is never entirely neutral and is shaped by the society it is developed in, as much as by scientific discovery. Technology is far more likely to receive investment and achieve widespread adoption under capitalism if it can produce more profit for capitalists, or more control for governments.

Within this argument, it is perhaps also worth considering the role of nuclear energy in any future energy mix. Nuclear energy seems very attractive in that it can replace the stable supply we currently rely on coal and gas for, $CO_2$ emissions are lower than for fossil fuels and in theory it is safe. In practice, however, we have seen poor government planning and capitalist corner-cutting cause pollution and incredibly high risk to life and pollution of the environment. Nuclear energy creates waste which remains active for many thousands of years and is very difficult to process and store safely. Furthermore, whilst often suggested to be a green energy source, the mining and enrichment of the required uranium are responsible for considerable emissions and risk the proliferation of material which would be used to make nuclear weapons. Within the current capitalist framework the profits from nuclear energy are privatised but the costs of the clean-up and the risks to the environment are socialised. Much hope is given to new reactors or nuclear fusion as a way to provide cheap and plentiful energy in the future. However, even if it were possible to deal with the risk of leaks and the spent fuel, nuclear energy is still a technology which requires immense resources to set up and run, and it is therefore incompatible with a decentralised, community-managed energy network. Even under our current political and economic system the costs are ridiculous. The UK's new power station, Hinkley C, is set to be the most expensive object ever built on land. Its spiralling costs make it a far worse deal than renewable alternatives. We are therefore sceptical of the role nuclear energy can play in a future society.

## Population Control

At a distance there is a cold logic to this idea. The number of people alive today is more than ever before, and surely fewer people would mean less pollution and lower $CO_2$ emissions? On closer inspection, this argument quickly falls apart for several reasons.

First and foremost is an idea examined in the excellent publication 'Too Many of Whom and Too Much of What?' by No One is Illegal. The 'whom' being talked about when this argument is made is always the poor, not the rich, and usually includes those that live in poorer countries or have migrated from them. Yet, it is disproportionately the richest people who are responsible for the most $CO_2$ emissions. Whilst this is most notable in the differences between rich and poor countries, it is also apparent between individuals within countries. The more unequal a society, the more carbon is emitted by the richest, and the more is emitted in total. You don't have to scratch the surface of this argument very hard to see it is rooted in racism and hatred of the poor, not in a genuine desire to help the planet.

Secondly, the idea contained within the 'population control' argument is that certain cultures have, and will always have, higher birth rates. This has been a common alarmist call by racists for over a century, who talk about native populations being 'swamped' by whichever group of people is currently the most vilified. In reality, every single population starts out at a stage of high birth rate and high death rate before moving through a stage of lowering death rate causing explosive growth. In the third stage the population rate slows down, before stabilising in the fourth stage. This is called 'The Demographic Transition', and it has happened or is happening in every human-inhabited area in the world. The average number of children born to each family globally has halved in the last 20 years. The things that help this transition are all things we should be fighting for in their own right, both in the here and now, and in any revolutionary future. Increased freedom, education and reproductive rights for women, better health care, stable food supplies and other increased standards of living. There is absolutely no rational argument to support restrictions or penalties from authority on those who choose to have more children because of the paternalistic idea that we need to 'teach' other cultures to have fewer children.

Finally, the population control argument assumes there is a direct link between increases/decreases in population and increases/decreases in capitalist growth and capitalist destruction of resources. However, as has already been discussed, capitalism requires maximum growth at all costs. Lowering the number of people on the planet would equally lower any meagre incentive capitalism creates for efficient or sustainable ways of working, and it would quickly restore or surpass previous levels of consumption and pollution.

# An Anarchist Ecology

We need a revolution that gets rid of the obstacles to implementing a planet-saving strategy. Many of the solutions already exist; it is a question of freeing the resources from the hands of capital and the state to implement them. The anarchist tradition has a rich history of ecological thought from Kropotkin and Reclus in the late nineteenth and early twentieth centuries, to Bookchin and Morris in more recent times. In this section we discuss why a future society based on anarchist communism offers a more sustainable future.

**Work.** The complete overhaul of the concept of work will affect every aspect of our lives and how our society is run. Less work and lower production will decrease the demand on energy and transportation networks. With less of our time devoted to work, journeys will be less urgent and will allow the sharing of transport and the use of more sustainable mass transportation methods rather than the current individual solutions such as car ownership. See the Anarchist Federation's pamphlet *Work* for more discussion on this topic.

**Production.** The current model of production for profit wastes vast amounts of resources, producing things we do not need and/or products that are designed for obsolescence and a short usable life, meaning we have to buy more and consume more. A shift in focus to production for societal need and products which can be repaired and maintained, will vastly lower the overall demand for resources. Alongside this, entire sectors of the economy will have no place in a future society; everything from advertising to the military industrial complex can be removed, freeing up resources to develop our transport and energy systems for the benefit of the people. Without speculation causing fluctuations in food and housing prices, products will reflect only their value in resources and their environmental impact, not the profits of capitalists.

**Intellectual property.** By abolishing intellectual property, laws, and the private ownership of the means of production, the best and most sustainable technologies will be adopted worldwide, skipping the carbon-intensive development model MEDCs have already been through. It will also encourage the best combination of components and technologies that were previously proprietary and owned by competing corporations.

**Sharing economy.** This term has been hijacked by tech start-ups and has come to mean the monetisation of things like 'homestays'. However, true communal ownership of tools and the building of shared resource facilities as an integral part of housing planning would allow communities to repair and maintain their homes without the need for each individual to own a lawn-mower or a power drill. Proper sharing of the means of transport like electric cars or bikes will mean lower demand for production and flexibility for individuals, as well as an effective mass transportation system. In short, people would not own as many assets individually but would reorganise life according to need i.e. communism.


**Food.** There have been a number of academic studies which have shown that we are able to feed a growing population without resorting to either intensive pesticide and herbicide use or deforestation (see *Nature Communications:* Bibliography). This task becomes even easier if there is a shift to more plant-based diets that require less land, energy and water inputs. Ultimately, food production is linked to land ownership and as long as this is in the hands of a few corporations the most profitable, and often least healthy, products will be pushed onto the consumer. Capitalism is so efficient that half of all food that is farmed is wasted. We imagine a world where land is held in common, and food production is localised as much as possible and focussed on providing abundant, healthy food with as minimal an impact on the environment as possible.

Unfortunately, the environmental crisis cannot wait for a revolution to destroy capitalism, nor will a post-revolutionary society be environmentally sound unless we manage to change the relationship between humans and the rest of nature. As anarchists we need to be doing everything we can to bring these issues to the forefront. We have identified a number of approaches to this.

1. We must make the link between capitalism and environmental degradation explicit in our politics and critique the role of the state in facilitating this. This pamphlet is a first step towards this, but we also need to work towards the dissemination of these ideas in the wider movement.

2. We must insert ourselves into the mass climate movements such as divestment, climate marches and third sector campaigns to use these moments of publicity to put forward our ideas. We should try to win the battle of ideas in these movements and shift the aims away from the false solutions identified here.

3. We must push our unions to adopt an eco-syndicalist stance which argues for a just but rapid transition for workers in extractive industries. We must also, however, be internationalist in our scope and ensure victories for workers in MEDCs does not mean just pushing environmental problems onto workers in LEDCs.

4. We must use our anti-capitalist analysis to link up different struggles, so that it is clear that we are not facing disconnected problems, but that capitalism is at the heart of the issues that face the global working class. Land justice campaigns have a clear link to climate change as land owners decide how land is used and how resources are exploited, counter to a sustainable commons approach. Similarly, we have identified rising nationalism and authoritarianism as the state's response to climate refugees. We must continue the work linking anti-capitalism and environmentalism with No Borders and migrant rights groups, ensuring the fair treatment of those affected by climate change in the future.

5. We must develop networks of like-minded people who are willing to campaign on these issues and work together to build our capacity to organise. A good example of this has been the anti-fracking protests in the UK where actions at the drilling sites have been amplified by activists elsewhere targeting the headquarters of the fracking companies and carrying out other solidarity actions. Some of these networks already exist so we should work more closely with groups such as Earth First!, Reclaim the Power and Rising Tide to further develop an activism which is both confrontational towards capitalism and is inclusive of local and global perspectives. These networks offer opportunities to develop our ideas further and collaborate on future projects and actions.

6. We should ensure the actions we take, and the struggles we link up for, leave us and others who take part stronger not weaker. We must avoid any so-called victory that relies on the 'good will' of a politician or the 'expertise' of an NGO. Win or lose, each action and campaign should leave us more aware of the world around us, more confident of our collective power, and more experienced in our ability to self-organise and take the fight to the capitalists. Within the environmental movement we must develop a diversity of tactics that is not dependent on the actions of politicians or corporations developing a conscience to achieve its goals.

# Conclusion

We are entering uncharted territory, in terms of how the earth's ecosystems may respond to the ever increasing pressures capitalism places upon them. Left unchecked, the current fossil fuel economy will continue to wreck the climate with the burden on impacts falling on the working class and LEDCs. We do not have faith that capitalists – or their parliamentarian representatives – will act in time to limit climate change in a meaningful way. The crisis they perpetuate can only lead to an increase in state control of the economy, of our lives, of the borders, as the ruling class seeks to contain social unrest and keep out climate refugees.

As anarchists, we see the only alternative to be a revolution from below, a revolution that begins in the struggles that we fight and win in this very moment. A world in which we take back control of our energy and production systems to create a new model of equality between peoples and harmony with nature. We see our future in the commons; we see our future in the beauty of anarchy.

# Bibliography

*The Green Zone: The Environmental Cost of Militarism*, Barry Sanders, AK Press, 2009

*A-Z of Green Capitalism*, Corporate Watch

*To the Ends of the Earth: A Guide to Unconventional Fossil Fuels*, Corporate Watch

*Too Many Of Whom And Too Much Of What?*, No One Is Illegal, 2010
*Work*, UK Anarchist Federation

*20 Theses Against Green Capitalism*, Tadzio Müller and Alexis Passadakis, 2009

Exploring the biophysical option space for feeding the world without deforestation, published open access in *Nature Communications*, 2016

Good Intents, but Low Impacts: Diverging Importance of Motivational and Socioeconomic Determinants Explaining Pro-Environmental Behavior, Energy Use, and Carbon Footprint, published in *Environment and Behaviour*, 2017

*Ecology and Socialism*, Brian Morris, 2010

*The Ecology of Freedom*, Murray Bookchin, 1982

Assessing ExxonMobil's climate change communications (1977–2014), published open access in *Environmental Research Letters,* 2017